Is Your Dog Jewish?

Leo Dworken

RUNNING PRESS
Philadelphia, Pennsylvania

Canadian representatives: General Publishing Co., Ltd.,
30 Lesmill Road, Don Mills, Ontario M3B 2T6.

International representatives: Worldwide Media Services, Inc.,
115 East Twenty-third Street, New York, New York 10010.

9 8 7 6 5 4 3 2 1

Digit on the right indicates the number of this printing.

Library of Congress Cataloging-in-Publication Number
89–43020

ISBN 0–89471–746–4

Cover design by Toby Schmidt
Interior design by Judith Barbour Osborne

This book may be ordered by mail from the publisher.
Please add $2.50 for postage and handling for each copy.
But try your bookstore first!
Running Press Book Publishers
125 South Twenty-second Street
Philadelphia, Pennsylvania 19103

For Aron Ben Tanchume

Acknowledgments

Many thanks to Lawrence Teacher, who first suggested the idea for this book, and to all those friends and colleagues who contributed ideas and questions, especially Alan Formanowitz, Rabbi Susan Harris, and Mark Kramer. I also want to thank the many who listened politely to questions in the early stages, including Frank Costello, Barbara Blake, Joellen Brown, Betty Lancaster, Sarah Babaian, Bruce Schimmel, and Kelly Crimmins.

My editor, Steven Zorn, proved invaluable both in suggesting topics for questions and in adding nuances and refinements.

To everyone who helped, I can only say, "Sei Gesund!"

Introduction

Questions are a particularly Jewish addiction. From Talmudic times, Jews have developed a tradition of asking questions to find out about themselves and others. I often find myself answering one question with another, using the ever-versatile Yiddish inflection of my grandparents to let the asker know just exactly what I think of a query.

When I first considered putting together a book of Jewish questions, I decided to start with all my relatives' favorite questions, ones that, to me, brilliantly expose the absurdity of modern life:

Nu?

When already?

Why so fancy-schmancy?

What am I, chopped liver?

Why me?

From that he makes a living?

But, alas, these questions seemed virtually unanswerable, and that was not my goal in compiling this little book. I wanted to find questions that would have many answers for many people, questions that would encourage reflection and discussion about what it is really like to be Jewish in America today.

You can use this book in many ways: alone, to discover more about yourself; with a loved one, to encourage the kind of intimate discussion we all get too little of these days; or in a group or at a party, to stimulate conversation that's guaranteed to go beyond normal small talk. The questions cover all facets of Jewish identity, from the most trivial to the most profound.

But enough already with the explanations. The book should speak for itself. So, enjoy—and ask!

1 **A**re you flattered or insulted when someone says you don't look Jewish?

2 **I**f your child asked, ''Why are we the chosen people?'' how would you respond?

3 Do you check movie credits for Jewish names? At a party, do you feel uncomfortable if you are the only Jew in the room? When are you most aware of being Jewish?

4 If you were a Nazi hunter, would you feel justified using illegal means to catch your prey?

5 Has anyone in your family had a nose job? How do you feel about Jews who have cosmetic surgery to look less Jewish?

6

If you were a renowned liver cancer specialist, the only doctor able to diagnose and treat a life-threatening illness of Moammar Qaddafi, would you agree to be flown to Libya to attend to him?

7 What is the best *mitzvah* anyone has ever performed for you? What is the best *mitzvah* you have performed for others?

8 If you were a famous singer who happened to be Jewish, would you record a Christmas album? What if you knew it would sell a million copies?

9 Do you feel that your parents were uncomfortable being Jewish, or did they instill ethnic pride in their children?

10 Who is the biggest *goniff* you've ever met?

Would you consider any of the following people Jewish?

A. A person raised as a Christian who has never formally converted to Judaism but lights Sabbath candles, attends synagogue, and keeps kosher.

B. A person born to observant Jewish parents but who observes no religious holidays or traditions.

C. A person from a Jewish family who attends synagogue only during the high holy days, has a Christmas tree, and does not keep kosher.

12 How would a private detective visiting your home be able to tell that a Jewish person lives there?

13 What's the most peculiar gentile custom you can think of?

14 What taste or smell triggers a Jewish memory?

15 What do you value most about being Jewish? What do you like least about it?

16 Do you believe that the Palestinians are entitled to a state of their own? If so, where do you think it should be located?

17

In Jewish wedding ceremonies, the parents of both the bride and the groom accompany the couple to the *chuppa*; in gentile marriages, only the father or parents of the bride are involved in the ''giving away'' of a child. Do you think the Jewish custom is better?

18

Do you believe that Japanese-Americans should have been reimbursed for the damages and injuries they suffered when they were detained in concentration camps during World War II?

19 Have you ever sung Christmas carols?

20 Do you know both of your grandmothers' maiden names?

21 Would you allow your high-school-age son or daughter to spend a summer in the occupied West Bank settlements in Israel?

Do you feel that there is a class system within American Jewry? For example, are German-American Jews wealthier or better educated on the whole than American Jews from Eastern Europe?

If you were at the airport, about to leave on a plane to Israel, and found out that a jet had just exploded on its way from Jerusalem to London, would you cancel your trip?

24 Do you believe that Jews who commit suicide should be allowed a Jewish burial? **25** Did your grandparents ever tell you that, in the Old Country, there were rabbis or aristocrats in your family? Do you believe them?

26 One psycho-historical theory holds that blonde women became movie sex symbols because Jewish heads of the movie studios were attracted to non-Jewish "bad" girls, or *shiksas*. Do you think this is true?

27 If you had been Noah, would you have been able to build the ark yourself? If you had to hire a contractor, how would you make sure he finished in time?

28 When was the last time you heard an anti-Semitic remark from a stranger? From a friend? Did you confront these people?

29 Would you allow your son or daughter to join the Israeli army?

30 If a law were passed in the United States requiring all Jews to register at their local police station, would you comply, or would you consider leaving the country? What if you had to give up all your assets to leave the country?

31 Do you believe in an afterlife? If so, how would a Jewish afterlife be different from a Christian afterlife? Do you think you would only be able to see your Jewish friends and relatives in the afterlife?

32 In what way do you think you most disappointed your parents?

33 If you were to win an all-expense-paid three-week trip to either Paris or Jerusalem, which would you choose?

34

What was your family name in the Old Country? If it was different from your surname, do you ever wish your relatives had kept it, or would you find it unwieldy or embarrassing?

You are having a pleasant dinner with a potential business client who is about to sign a contract that would bring your company four million dollars. Over brandy and coffee, she explains her theory that Jews control all of the world's banks and media and that they are about to take over the government. Would you voice your objection to what she is saying, or would you keep silent to procure the contract?

36 Do you think Jews have a better sense of humor than non-Jews? How does Jewish humor differ from gentile humor?

37 How do you feel about Jews who have Christmas trees? If you're Jewish and have a Christmas tree, how do you justify it to your Jewish friends who complain?

38 Which would be more upsetting to your parents: that you never marry, or that you marry outside the faith? What if you were to convert to marry outside the faith?

39 If you and your mate desperately wanted a child but knew that any child of yours had a fifty percent chance of having Tay-Sachs disease, would you still try to conceive?

40

If there were a candidate running for an important office who believed in essentially the same things you did, but was known to have made a series of anti-Semitic remarks, would you vote for him or her? What if the same candidate spoke badly about another minority instead of Jews—would you vote for the candidate then?

41 Do you think that Jews will exist as a distinct group one thousand years from now? How about five hundred years from now?

42 Statistics indicate that one out of every three Jews marries out of the faith. Do you believe that intermarriage is destroying the Jewish religion?

43 Do you fast on Yom Kippur? If not, when and why did you stop?

44 Do Jews make good lovers? Was the most satisfying sexual experience you ever had with a Jewish or a non-Jewish partner?

45 Would you choose to be cremated, even though it is against Jewish law and might upset your relatives?

46 Would you refuse to watch a television show if an actor in the cast had made anti-Semitic remarks in a public interview? Would you write a letter to the producers?

47 What is the fondest memory you have of your *Bubbe* or *Zayde*?

48 If your mate decided to become Orthodox, do you think you could go on living with him or her?

49 Do you feel that some aspect of your personality fits a Jewish stereotype? Is this a negative or positive stereotype?

Have you ever felt uncomfortable at church weddings or on other occasions when you have found yourself in a Christian church or cathedral? If you had a rule of never setting foot inside a church, would you break it to be best man or maid of honor at your best friend's wedding?

51 Can the Holocaust ever happen again?

52 Do you agree with the phrase, "Hope for the best, expect the worst"? Are Jews typically pessimists?

53

When buying something, do you haggle over the price? Do you think that bargaining with a salesperson reinforces a Jewish stereotype? Are you more likely to bargain than your non-Jewish friends?

54 Can you name all five Marx brothers and describe what they looked like?

55 If you were given $50,000 to write an enthusiastic blurb for the jacket of a book by Yasir Arafat, would you do it?

56 Are you more sexually attracted to non-Jews or Jews? Some psychologists say that an attraction to other ethnic groups indicates self-loathing—do you agree?

57 If you became very ill and needed a specialist, would you feel more comfortable with a Jewish doctor?

58 If the Christmas season were suddenly to disappear, how would you feel?

D 59 **o** you feel that certain jobs or professions are stereotypically Jewish? How about your own job?

60 **W** ho is your favorite Jewish author? Do you prefer Jewish writers over non-Jewish ones?

61 Do you know the words to any Chanukah songs? Do you believe that Chanukah is only a minor holiday that has been ''hyped'' in order to compete with Christmas?

62 When choosing between two unfamiliar candidates, are you more likely to vote for someone with a Jewish name?

63 Was the casting of Charlton Heston, a non-Jew, to play Moses the same as casting a Westerner to play Charlie Chan?

64 Is an Orthodox Jew ''more Jewish'' than a Conservative or Reform Jew, or do followers of these branches merely express their Judaism in different, but ''equally Jewish'' ways?

65 If you were a heart surgeon with two infant patients, one Jewish and one non-Jewish, who were waiting for organs, would you give the first heart to the Jewish child?

66 Does it especially bother you if a Jewish person commits a heinous crime?

67 Have you ever done anything that would make your grandparents roll over in their graves?

68 If you adopted a child, would you want the child to undergo a formal conversion to Judaism? If the child were a male toddler, would you have him circumcised?

69 Do you think Sandy Koufax should have pitched in the World Series on Yom Kippur?

70 If you had a son who was admitted to medical school at age thirteen but had to skip his bar mitzvah in order to become a doctor, would you let him go?

71 If you were a Nazi war criminal who found yourself reincarnated as a Jew, with total recollection of your past life, how would you atone for your crimes?

You are allowed to go back in time to change one event in history. Would you choose to alter the destiny of the Jewish people in any way?

73 Do you believe that women should be rabbis? Would you want your daughter to be a rabbi? How do you feel when you see a woman in a yarmulke and prayer shawl?

74 How often have you been drunk in your life? Do you agree with the stereotype that Jews don't drink?

75 Would you want lots of money, a fancy house, and the career of your dreams if the price you had to pay was three unhappy marriages, or would you rather have one happy marriage with barely enough money to scrape by?

76 Do you believe that Jews are, on the whole, the smartest ethnic group in this country?

77 If somehow nature were changed and you were forced to derive all your nourishment from one traditional Jewish food, which would you choose?

78 Are the majority of your friends Jewish or non-Jewish? Why do you think that is?

79 If you were given a free week at a hotel in the Catskills or Miami Beach, which would you choose?

80 When you go to a *bris,* do you watch the actual surgery on the infant? Do you think circumcision should be performed in this way, or in a hospital?

81 If you needed an organ transplant, would you want a Jewish donor? **82** Do you believe that people should give baby gifts before a baby is born, or that the parents should set up the baby's room before the birth? If not, why not?

83 Where do you plan to retire? Would it matter to you if there wasn't a sizable Jewish population there?

84 Would you move to a very small town where you knew you could never get good delicatessen food?

W 85 ho's the most Jewish person you know?

86 **O** rthodox Jewish law states that a child's mother must be Jewish in order for the child to be considered a Jew. Would you accept the child of a Jewish father and gentile mother as a Jew?

Some insurance companies are refusing to reimburse for circumcision. If circumcision were outlawed in the United States, would you still have your son circumcised? What if circumcision were definitely proved medically dangerous for babies? What if the operation simply became unfashionable, and your son would look "different" in the locker room?

88 When were you first aware that you were Jewish, or that other people weren't? **89** If you could attend a Seder in the company of five other Jews, living or dead, whom would you choose?

Which traditional Jewish food gives you the most indigestion? Do you still eat it? Why do you think Jewish food is so heavy? Did all of our ancestors walk around with heartburn?

If a friend were fixing you up with a blind date, would you feel better knowing that the date was Jewish? What if, upon meeting the person, you discovered he or she was extremely devout (i.e., observed strict dietary laws, wouldn't drive on the Sabbath, etc.)? If, in all other respects, you and this person were compatible, could you see yourself falling in love?

92 Who is your favorite Jewish athlete? Why do you think there are so few Jewish professional athletes?

93 If you were to marry out of the faith, would you insist that your children be raised as Jews?

94 All Jews are legally allowed to emigrate to Israel, but there is a movement to exclude Conservative, Reform, and Reconstructionist converts to Judaism from that privilege. Do you believe that converts are "real" Jews? If so, would you accept a convert as a rabbi?

95 What is the tackiest bar mitzvah reception you have ever attended? If you were given carte blanche to pick any location for a bar mitzvah party, where would you select?

In what ways did your mother fit the stereotype of a Jewish mother? In what ways was she different? What's the funniest thing she ever said to you?

97 Whose movies do you prefer, Mel Brooks's or Woody Allen's? Which director/actor seems more Jewish to you?

98 What is your favorite Jewish holiday, and how do you celebrate it?

99 If you have pets, do you think of them as Jewish? **100** Do you resent it when people ask if you are Jewish? What do you say?

101 Are Jewish parents more concerned with their children's education than non-Jewish parents? Did your parents push you toward a particular profession?

102 Do you think of Sammy Davis, Jr., as Jewish? What about Elizabeth Taylor?

When a Jew and a Christian get married and neither converts to the other's religion, do you think they should choose a judge or justice of the peace as officiant? Or do you think they should try to find a priest and a rabbi who will officiate together?

104 "In spite of everything, I still believe that people are really good at heart." These words were written by Anne Frank, a Holocaust victim. Do you think they're true?

105 If you had to pretend not to be Jewish for a year in order to take advantage of the job opportunity of a lifetime, would or could you do it?

Have you ever bought a German car or other major consumer product? Would you travel in Germany? Would you tell your older relatives that you had?

If you could spend a day with one figure from the Old Testament— Adam, Eve, Moses, Abraham, David, Noah, Judith, Esther, etc.— which person would you choose?

On which holidays do you send cards—Rosh Hashanah, Chanukah, or Christmas? If you send Christmas cards, do you always choose ones that say "Season's Greetings?" Do you get insulted if someone sends you a "Merry Christmas" message?

109 In what incident from your life did you display the greatest amount of *chutzpah*?

110 Which do you think is worse—Catholic guilt or Jewish guilt? Therapists say that Catholics are guilty mostly about sex. What are Jews guilty about?

If you and your family had to flee America, but you could only afford passage for half of your family, whom would you send?

W 112

hat are three professions you would be amazed to find a Jew involved in? The Pope and other non-Jewish religious figures don't count.

113 If you could live your life all over again, would you choose to be born Jewish?

114 In *Stardust Memories,* Woody Allen talks about his mother putting the chicken through the "deflavorizing machine." What is the worst recipe your mother cooked when you were growing up?

115 You are traveling on an airliner that is hijacked by Palestinian terrorists. The terrorist leader rounds up all passengers from your section and tells the group that he will shoot everyone unless one Jew steps forward. Would you identify yourself as a Jew, not knowing what would happen to you?

116 Who is the biggest *schnorrer* you have ever met?

117 Are you more likely to buy a car or major appliance from a store owned by Jews?

If you had to choose between having a mental condition that would take five years of intensive psychotherapy to remedy or a serious physical condition that would require corrective surgery with an 85% survival rate, which would you choose?

119 Have you ever been in a place where you felt that people treated you in an unfriendly manner because you are Jewish?

120 Did your parents follow the Ashkenazi custom of naming you for a dead relative? If so, what was the relative's name? Do you know anything about him or her? Would you follow the custom in naming your own children? How is it done in your family — using the Hebrew name, or using only a first initial?

W **121**
hy is New York City the most Jewish city on earth? **122** D o you consider yourself a religious person? If so, how often do you attend *shul*? Would you want a Jewish funeral?

123 Have you ever killed an animal for sport? Do you think of hunting as a non-Jewish pastime?

124 Did you ever have your picture taken with Santa Claus or the Easter Bunny?

125 If you had always considered yourself Jewish and then discovered that your great-grandmother was not Jewish, would it alter your ethnic identity in any way?

Would you ever consider living with your child when you become elderly? If you already have children, with which one would you choose to live? Could you ever imagine having one or both of your parents come to live with you?

127 Do you eat non-kosher foods? If so, do you do so in front of parents or other relatives?

128 Would you be more upset if your daughter married out of the faith, or if your son did so?

129 Do you consider Jewish jokes offensive if told by Jews? What if they are told by gentiles? What is the most offensive Jewish joke you've ever heard?

If studies showed that each Jew had to have five children in order to keep the Jews from becoming extinct, would you plan a large family?

131 Can you recite all Ten Commandments? How many have you broken in your lifetime? Do you think they are still relevant? **132** Do you think of Jesus Christ as Jewish?

133

How old were you before you realized that there was no such thing as a gefilte fish that swam in the sea?

134 You are suddenly transported back to late-nineteenth-century Poland. Could you muster enough Yiddish to make yourself understood when asking for food or shelter?

135 If you had a son and a daughter, would it seem more tragic to you if your son never succeeded at his profession than if your daughter failed to achieve success at hers?

136

According to one definition, a *schlemiel* is a guy who spills his soup; a *schlamazel* is the guy he spills it on. In the great game of life, are you a *schlemiel* or a *schlamazel* ?

W 137

Who is the best
kibbitzer you know?

138 **A**re you or any
of your relatives
Republicans? Why do
you think there are so few
Republican Jews?

139 If you found out that your next door neighbor, with whom you had been very friendly, belonged to the Ku Klux Klan, would you still talk to him over the fence?

140 If you could choose to marry one famous Jewish person, who would it be? If you could choose to spend one night in bed with a famous Jewish person, would it be the same person?

141 How do you feel about Jews for Jesus, or Messianic Jews? Do you think that people who accept Jesus Christ as a savior have a right to call themselves Jews?

Are Jews more neurotic than gentiles? Do you think it is a coincidence that modern psychoanalysis was invented by a Jew, Sigmund Freud?

143 If a black family moved next door, would you allow your daughter to date one of their sons?

144 What is the strangest superstition your family holds? Did your parents or grandparents ever talk about the Evil Eye?

145 Which would you prefer: that your child make an unhappy marriage and provide you with grandchildren, or that your child never marry at all?

146 If you caught the fourteen-year-old son of a close non-Jewish friend defacing your synagogue and he begged you not to turn him over to the police, what would you do?

147 Are Jews more tolerant of other minorities than non-Jews? **148** Is there one food or drink you love yet your non-Jewish friends won't touch?

149 Do you think that Ethel and Julius Rosenberg were guilty of treason and should have been executed, or do you believe that they were victims of anti-Semitism?

150 Would you feel comfortable attending a service in a gay synagogue? How would you feel if you found out your own rabbi was gay?

151 What would you say if someone wished you a "Happy Yom Kippur"?

152 Would you emigrate to Israel if you knew you could make a living there?

153

Does it bother you that the first Jewish Miss America, Bess Myerson, was later prosecuted on grounds of bribing a judge and also was arrested for shoplifting?

154 Who is the biggest *kvetch* you know? Have you ever told him or her that you're sick of hearing the complaints?

155 If research showed that eating pork three times a day would prolong anyone's life by ten years, would you feel comfortable doing it?

156 When you are in distress, do you ever reflexively use a Yiddish expression, such as *"Oy vey,"* *"goyische kop,"* or (pointing to your head) *"tuches"*?

157 When you were growing up, did you ever want to be a Christian?

A 158

A cab driver who doesn't realize you are Jewish strikes up a conversation about a television movie depicting the Holocaust. He tells you that he doesn't really believe that six million Jews were killed, that it is a lie perpetrated by the Jewish media. What would you say to him, if anything?

159 Who tells the worst jokes in your family? **160** Can an atheist be Jewish?

161 Do you speak differently to Jews than to non-Jews? Do you find yourself using more hand gestures, speaking about different subjects, or interjecting more Yiddish than when speaking to gentile friends?

162 If the Messiah were to arrive tomorrow, what do you think he'd say about Judaism? Do you think he would keep kosher?

163 Do you know anyone who's Jewish who doesn't like Chinese food?

164

What is your Hebrew name? Do you know what it means?

165 What's the stupidest thing anyone's ever said to you about being Jewish?

There are many Jewish folktales about *golem,* robot-like creatures created by people to perform simple tasks. If you could create a *golem,* what would it be like, what would you name it, and what tasks would you want it to perform?

167 What is your favorite Yiddish word? Did you learn it as a child? **168** Does God have a Jewish sense of humor?

169 Do you have personal proof that chicken soup can cure colds?

170 If you could write your own *ketubah* (marriage contract), specifying everything you would want in a relationship, what would you include?

171 How can you tell if a person is a real *mensh*? Do you believe that you are a *mensh*?

172 If you only had time to volunteer for one charitable organization, would you choose a Jewish organization?

173 If your child came home from school and said that a classmate had called him a "dirty Jew," what would you advise him to do?

174 Who's the worst *yenta* you know? What's the worst story he or she ever told you?

175 Do you enjoy popularizations of Jewish culture, such as *Fiddler on the Roof* and *Yentl,* or do you find them schmaltzy?

Who was the first of your family to arrive in America? Who was the last? Do you know what part of the Old Country they came from? Do you know the details of their first years in America?

When you take time off from work on Jewish holidays, do you attend synagogue? If not, do you feel guilty?

178 If you could erect any sort of monument to the six million Jews lost in the Holocaust, what would it be like, and where would you locate it?

179 Are the words *shiksa* and *goy* as offensive as *yid* and *kike*?

180 If your child had a choice of taking German, French, or Hebrew in school, which would you advise? **181** Do you know all the words to "Haveh Nagileh" and "Hatikvah"? Do you know what they mean?

If you were a Soviet Jew, would you choose to emigrate to Israel or the U.S., knowing that you would never see your friends and relatives again?

183

If you could go back in time to advise your family on where to settle when they came to the United States, which city or area would you recommend?

184 Were girls treated differently than boys in your family? In general, do you think Judaism is a sexist religion?

185 Would you vote for a presidential candidate who was not pro-Israel?

186 Methuselah lived more than nine hundred years. How long would you like to live, and in what manner would you prefer to die?

187 Would you tell your parents or other relatives how much you make per year? How about your friends?

The Bible specifically prohibits Jews from settling in Egypt, where they were once enslaved. Would you consider visiting Egypt? How would you feel if your daughter decided to become an Egyptologist?

189
If someone said to you, ''Your people killed our Lord,'' how would you respond?

190
What makes the Jewish people so resilient?

191 When you have made a right decision, do you feel it in your *kishkas*?

192 Should neo-Nazi groups have the right to hold public parades in the United States?

193 If you were a famous trial attorney, would you defend a fundamentalist Christian preacher accused of murder if you knew he was innocent? How about if you knew he was guilty?

194 What do you think is the most Jewish aspect of your appearance? Why?

195 If you had no living relatives, which friend would you choose to say *kaddish* over you at your funeral?

Who do you think will be elected president of the United States first: a woman, a black, or a Jew? Do you think there will ever be a Jewish president? If so, how many years do you predict before it will happen? Of all the prominent Jews today, who would make the best president?

197 Do you consider yourself a Zionist? Do you believe that the Jews were entitled to a homeland after the Holocaust?

198 If you had a choice of living in identical houses in either a Jewish neighborhood or a non-Jewish neighborhood, which would you choose?

199 How would your parents answer the questions in this book?